T0032117

AFTER THAT

ALSO BY LORNA CROZIER

POETRY
Inside Is the Sky (1976)
Crow's Black Joy (1979)
No Longer Two People (with Patrick Lane) (1979)
Humans and Other Beasts (1980)
The Weather (1983)
The Garden Going On Without Us (1985)
Angels of Flesh, Angels of Silence (1988)
Inventing the Hawk (1992)
Everything Arrives at the Light (1995)
A Saving Grace (1996)
What the Living Won't Let Go (1999)
Apocrypha of Light (2002)
Bones in Their Wings: Ghazals (2003)
Whetstone (2005)
The Blue Hour of the Day: Selected Poems (2007)
Small Mechanics (2011)
The Book of Marvels: A Compendium of Everyday Things (2012)
The Wrong Cat (2015)
The Wild in You: Voices from the Forest and the Sea (2015)
What the Soul Doesn't Want (2017)
God of Shadows (2018)
The House the Spirit Builds (2019)
After That (2023)

ANTHOLOGIES
A Sudden Radiance (with Gary Hyland) (1987)
Breathing Fire (with Patrick Lane) (1995)
Desire in Seven Voices (2000)
Addicted: Notes from the Belly of the Beast (with Patrick Lane) (2001)
Breathing Fire 2 (with Patrick Lane) (2004)

NON-FICTION
Small Beneath the Sky (2009)
Through the Garden (2020)

FOR CHILDREN
Lots of Kisses (2014)
So Many Babies (2015)
More Than Balloons (2017)

After That

Poems

LORNA CROZIER

McClelland & Stewart

Copyright © 2023 by Lorna Crozier

First edition published 2023

McClelland & Stewart and colophon are registered trademarks of
Penguin Random House Canada Limited.

All rights reserved. The use of any part of this publication reproduced, transmitted in
any form or by any means, electronic, mechanical, photocopying, recording, or otherwise,
or stored in a retrieval system, without the prior written consent of the publisher—
or, in case of photocopying or other reprographic copying, a licence from the Canadian
Copyright Licensing Agency—is an infringement of the copyright law.

Published simultaneously in the United States of America.

Library and Archives Canada Cataloguing in Publication

Title: After that : poems / Lorna Crozier.
Names: Crozier, Lorna, 1948- author.
Identifiers: Canadiana 20230157971 | ISBN 9780771004285 (softcover) |
    ISBN 9780771004292 (EPUB)
Classification: LCC PS8555.R72 A78 2023 | DDC C811/.54—dc23

Cover design by Talia Abramson
Cover art: Rachel Claire / pexels.com
Typeset in Dante by M&S, Toronto
Printed in Canada

McClelland & Stewart,
a division of Penguin Random House Canada Limited,
a Penguin Random House Company
www.penguinrandomhouse.ca

1 2 3 4 5   27 26 25 24 23

Penguin
Random House
McCLELLAND & STEWART

With love, for my husband, Patrick Lane,
b. March 26, 1939, d. March 7, 2019

CONTENTS

Love, the final loss, the last
giving.

JOHN THOMPSON, *Stilt Jack*

my words spare as the seeds of poverty grass
that fall on wasted ground.

PATRICK LANE, *The Quiet in Me*

AFTER THAT

AFTER

In some countries the young men
shave their heads, the women cut their hair
so it doesn't fall below the chin.
In some countries mirrors are draped
with black cloths stored in a trunk for this purpose
alone. In some, if death comes in winter,
all the bereaved can use as fuel
are the shadows of birches
the oldest in the family
gathers from the snow and breaks
into kindling for a fire
as cold, as blue
as after.

PATIENCE

The heron at the edge of the pond
at dawn. You have to remind yourself
he isn't bamboo sticks and glued-on feathers
but the real thing, more patient than a monk
which he resembles with his scoliotic
shoulder shrug, his smooth grey head,
legs skinny and naked jutting from a robe
the wind just lifted. You are learning his ways, not moving
until he moves, emptying yourself of everything
but the mind's reflection, a thoughtless
thinking, a blue on blue
the koi slip through.

LET THERE BE ANGELS

William Blake heard angels singing.
I wonder what you heard at the end.
The trauma doctor said, *Talk to him if you want,*
he can hear you. This was before he turned off
the machine. I talked to you between kisses,
I kissed your mouth, your eyes, lowered the sheet
and kissed your chest and belly,
I took your long feet in my hands and kissed your toes
and the pale soles mapped with where you'd walked
for almost eighty years. I took the palms
of your hands and laid them on me, the last time
they would touch me, I held each hand between mine
the way I'd hold a broken bird, I talked, I didn't say anything
that would surprise you, but my mouth was busy—maybe
you weren't pleased, you wanted more; in times that mattered
we always tried to say something
the other didn't know.

WHEN I STOP SAYING YOUR NAME

The words of the old calligrapher
in Hangzhou

    the ink he made
    from water and ground
    graphite blackening his tongue:

where the brush strokes stop

        the snow begins

FIELD OF WHEAT

(After Ingeborg Bachmann)

When someone departs he must give his body to the field of wheat,
he must toss his sweaters, his old boots, his felt slippers
into the field of wheat, he must drive his truck
into the field until it runs out of gas, he must hurl his cutlery, his
    dishes, his hammers and saws,
he must toss his desk and all his books, even the volumes about
    gardening
into the field of wheat, he must bury his watch
between the stately rows, his wedding ring, his regrets, his promise
    to outlast,
he must blow the minutes he has left into the beards of wheat,
turn his other half, his shadow, into chaff;
it will be lifted by the wind, the wind that loves the wheat, the wind
that turns the field of wheat into a green and golden sea:
then and only then will the woman let him go, will she walk
the rows and rows and count the seeds of ripening wheat until she
    reaches
if she can, the number of her tears.

PARCEL

In the bag I carry from the crematorium
you weigh more than the heart of a horse.
How do I know how much that is?
I don't, but I say to myself,
You weigh more than the heart of a horse.

WHAT IS THE MOST YOU CAN ASK OF AIR?

Some see the departed standing in the doorway,
some say they are visited
in dreams. At night when the mattress gives

beside me it's not you but the cat
come in from hunting moths
along the lit pathways of the garden.

When I get up and open the curtains
a moth the size of my thumb
thuds and mutters against the glass.

Does the cat capture this ragged soul
to bring it back to me? If breath
had a shape it would be this moth,

huffing along the carpet,
grey and night-aware,
all you can ask of air.

ALMOST A CHILDREN'S STORY

One day you met a fox by the railroad tracks.
Both of you stopped in the tall grass
and looked at one another. Don't make a big deal
out of this, said the fox. I'm just a fox.
One day you met a magpie high in the spruce.
Both of you stayed still and looked at one another.
Don't make a big deal out of this, said the magpie.
I'm just a magpie. But if you want to help,
tell the monk to put away his rifle. I won't eat the robin's babies.
One day you met a snake between the raspberry bushes.
Both of you froze and looked at one another.
He'd been sipping the clear liquid
around the mouths of the bottles hidden
in the woodpile, the ivy, the brambles.
When he spoke he slurred and hissed.
It was hard for you to listen but you're sure he didn't say
I'm just a snake. Did this mean he was someone else,
it was a haunting, a visitation?
Why is it the bad days come back and not the good?

Take on another language, an alphabet of bone and sinew and grit. Chew the gristle and learn by heart the songbook's oldest song before you try to speak his name.

INSIDE A NEEDLE

This summer, night comes to her
as a large animal, breathing. Warm and damp
where its breath meets her skin.

Too much time near a sick bed
creates another sickness, sweats and chills
and a high fever for the past.

The deadless man lives inside a needle inside an egg
inside a duck inside a rabbit. That sounds right
though the folklore is not her own.

Don't say your life is ending.
There's a woman at your door
with three round loaves of bread.

The mind's gone soft from spending hours
on feather pillows. Who is forgetting you
so perfectly today?

ADAGIO ON THE DAY OF YOUR BIRTHDAY, THREE WEEKS AFTER YOU DIED

Do you remember in our first house,
Regina, Cathedral Avenue, the window open—
must have been late spring—we heard someone playing
a piano on the other side of the fence? How did we find out
it was the cat, a black-and-white walking the keys, a sad
C minor it went back to, over and over again?
We couldn't see through the window the cat. Who told us?
Must've been Robbie, the neighbour, who also owned
a mean dog, a female Rottweiler with a lopped-off tail.
Robbie ran down the rundown house and was dying,
we didn't know it then, of AIDS. The dog
who barked at everything fell quiet when the cat
made music. Delinquent birds flocked to the fence
as if to listen, scruffy sparrows in a row, tough guys with collars
turned up, and two house finches, red-capped, so much prettier
than the name they didn't choose. A tuxedo cat, remember?
His claws adding percussion like a wire brush stroking a tambourine.
This was years ago. I hold these sounds in a shadow chamber
in my inner ear where I hold your voice, the *sshush*
of your last breath, your slippers across the carpet,
the shuffle, and the pause, and the not going on.

NORTH OF WINTER

The dictionary word of the day is *ultima Thule*,
the land beyond the northernmost region on the maps.
Is that where you are now? Your poems loved winter.
Like the Mad Trapper are you walking backwards,
bone glasses over your eyes so you won't go blind?
You were before you died, going blind I mean, the straight
lines on a grid wavering when you looked close.
Macular degeneration, the doctor said, for which there is no cure.
May I say, now that my words cannot disturb you (we were so careful
near the end), you were dying though I could not see it then.
     In Saskatchewan
we drove through countless storms, your hands tight on the wheel,
snakes of snow slithering across the road, erasing the yellow line,
joining lane and ditch. That was the start perhaps,
your eyes blizzarded. In this north of north where I can't go,
your breath's come back and hangs in ice-flecked clouds
as you walk backwards into snow. Through narrow slits cut
into bone, bone is all you see.

FIELD GUIDE TO SILENCE

Some cat's
       got the grass's tongue.

       Wind nattering in aspen leaves
stutters into stillness.

Nothing more
       after that

A window on oiled hinges

up there in the sky
        slides open.

            Did a bird fly in, fly out,
                            what unfettered

        song?

Why do we assume
moths have no vernacular?

What delicate phonemes
could be fashioned

    from such thin
   extravagant tongues—

a lexicon of lick and taste,
of night-knowing,

      of sitting still
        and lapse

   their moth thoughts

  dusty and divinatory, the eyes

on their wings
   a lucid

 second sight.

Cold is a lump in the throat, an
      aphasia, a forgetting. Those childish

angels in the drifts,
        footless, with such blunt wings?

What you remember most
      is their muteness, all in a row.

Is it possible for hands
       to lose their language

their alphabets of finger
             and thumb?

The axe heard them,
the handle of the spade,
the wrench, the washing

hung on the line, the woman's
             naked shoulder and hip
heard them.

Now the palms and digits speak
       to nothing, to no one.
They palsy, they mumble,

          they dumb down.
Such a loss to the axe,
       to the spade, the wrench,

such a loss to the woman
       curled on one side of the bed

clothespin in her mouth.

The black-and-white cat
      buried in the yard

under the slate bench.
        She was quiet

when she was alive,
      imagine her now!

Moss grows a plush pelt above her
on this bench where she used to sit.

In the evening there, her mistress
      gently calls her name

  as if a soft-pawed ghost

waits in the shadows to draw near.
A late snow
settles in the woman's hair and in the moss

as if the moss too is growing old.

      ⌒

Under the water
        two turtles burrow into the muck

and no one

thinks of them
                        till spring

the pond a faceless
        pocket watch

faintly ticking

＿Ｏ

The stones around the pond
hold something
      close to their chests

  their heartbeats at rest
so far apart

you miss the lub / dub
      the yes, the no
  the altogether

and come to believe

there is nothing
    but stone
inside a stone.

Nothing's more quiet
      than the seeds

of
the cottonwood

      lighting on the pages
of an open book

on the hairs of the gardener's forearm
on the brown fur of a rabbit

      the rabbit the cat has
his eye on, that tense, muscled

      hush
            not even a whisker
of sound from prey
          or predator

      a fluff of seed drifting

through the air, touching
the tip of
the long twitching ear, settling

momentarily
        there

Repeat after Lorca, "Light doesn't know what it wants." But its opposite does. Darkness wants the spark you've carried since your birth to illuminate its path. Otherwise, no matter where it goes, it can't find its way.

WINTER'S GARDEN

Is there peace in the winter garden,
is there consolation? No weeds to pull,
nothing to be harvested, washed, and eaten.
The fish hang in the pond on strings
gelatinous with cold. The moss sinks
deep into itself. You, too, could go there,
to that giving up, that bedding down.
You are weary of who you are,
you are lonely. Like that tree rachitic
and bare. Like that box on a pole
your husband built for bats, but no bat
goes there. In memory of him, in hope
he still knows, a blunt-winged
leathery thing flies from your chest
to roost inside it, blood pooling
in your head. When night falls,
will you blunder from the opening and feed,
will you plush and fatten on winter's
poor abstractions, its scant repast?

EVENING SONG

Evening song from a bird you don't know,
sounding through the almost dark, never
darker until now, and you, nameless,
on your own, even more
so than before,
sing too.

HOW DID HE DIE?

1.
He ended up at Okanagan Lake.
Fashioned a paper boat and pushed it
from shore, a bracelet of
baby teeth inside it.

2.
His mother came in spirit
and carried him
mightily away. Small
in her arms and blond as he was
as a child. She didn't smell
of smoke and gin.

3.
We went together.

4.
He held a wounded gyrfalcon
in his left hand. It screamed
as its soul left its body.
He could feel the lightness
in his own chest.

5.
He died in his sleep.
There were no excrescences.
A dragonfly sat on his forehead,
its sharp feet gripping his skin.

6.
We went together.
It was a dream and we
both awakened, the five cats
we'd loved over forty years
restless in the bed.
One of us had to get up and feed them.
One of us couldn't be dead.

7.
Three a.m. Across the street
in the high reach of the trees
was the wind playing
a violin? Though mostly deaf
he turned his head toward
what he heard as music.
Listen—Lorna, listen!
the last words he said.

INSTRUCTIONS

(after Pier Paola Pasolini)

Loneliness: you must be strong to live
with it, take it into your bed, comb
its thinning hair with your fingers crook'd
before you douse the lamp. You must be unafraid
to answer the door, walk to the corner
over broken cement, welcome
the black dog and the crow who wait
every morning for your humble scraps.

You must ignore the pitiful eyes of shoppers
as you unpack for the cashier
the single lamb chop, the child's
fist of broccoli, the russet potato
wrapped in foil. In the study
you must read to the no one who is there
your favourite passage, at the stove
say *Taste this* and offer an empty spoon.

Every night, sleepy or not, you must
take loneliness into your bed,
slip lavender and sage beneath its pillow,
make sure your breath is sweet
when you turn your face toward it;
then begin the prayer that opens into silence
                    and ends with silence
and silence in between

MAN FROM THE DEATH INSTITUTE

(after Novica Tadić)

Stacks last year's letters
marked *Return to Sender*
in the locked box at the end
of your road where the streetlight's
been blown out.

Drops in the middle
of the white alyssum
a set of false teeth
the undertaker didn't
take under.

Posts an eviction notice
on the door of your study,
flips the books on the shelves
so their spines face the wall.

Hangs on the mountain ash
a feeder of such intricate design
the winged ones nightly gather,
golden beaks cracking seeds.

Soon they turn their heavenly
heads in your direction.
You wonder what
those dead eyes see.

Find the herb that grows on stone and brew it for tea.
It will make your heart turn hard.

HANGZHOU

It is raining in the garden Li Po
designed. How you would have loved it—
you knew Li Po by heart, you knew
the rain by heart and the beautiful woman
who was my guide, her ebony hair gleaming under
the red umbrella, you would have laughed
with her, I know, you would have recited Li Po.
Before my bed
there is bright moonlight
So that it seems
like frost on the ground.

If you'd been there with me,
I might have found tracks before dawn
outside your hut, the arch of her foot in frost,
the curve of the fallen moon.

I would have wound the long hair
from your pillow around my finger as a charm,
a thin black ring on my wedding finger
where I don't wear a ring anymore.
It would be okay, everything would be okay
if I could have you back.

THE NEW MUSIC

When the stroke paralyzed
his right side
from forehead to foot

his wife found
piano music
for the left hand.

I learn to walk
without you
talk to the

indifferent ear,
touch myself
with the dumber hand

fingers learning
the new music
someone who loved me

left for me to find
on the numb
side of the bed.

IN LIEU OF FLOWERS

When someone knocks on the door
pray he is not bearing
another bouquet of flowers

but an animal on a leash—
a goat would be best—
you can lead him

to the vases—the hall, the kitchen,
the living room,
the bed strewn with dying blooms—

such a beautiful feast—freesias
and chrysanthemums, rosebuds
and roses, the labia of orchids.

You love the stink of him,
the violence of his teeth,
the sound of his hoofs

throughout the house,
soft on the carpet,
hard on the hardwood floor.

CERBERUS

The dog you rescued
is not a rescue dog.
He doesn't need
to be saved, he doesn't
need to save anyone.

Even if he tracked you down,
buried in an avalanche, lost in the woods,
you'd be terrified and might choose to stay
in the trouble you were in.

A stray, he showed up on your porch,
lips curled back, his cavernous mouths
drooling, his six eyes bright as coals.

His job down there was to stop
the dead from leaving.

In your yard, on the streets,
within the walls of your city,
this is the work
you want him
to resume—

MY GRIEF

(after Zbigniew Herbert's "Our Fear")

My grief
does not drink its coffee sweet
does not look with grackle eyes
or ride a wild horse
through fields of burning barley.

My grief
fits into a paper sack
with a jackknife   an abacus of knuckle bones
a travel cup of whisky   a small brown bat.
When the bag tears on the journey
it's the abacus that flies away,
knuckles cracking.

My grief
does not need shoes and shelter
does not need a mother
or another heart to use for parts.

My grief covers itself with soot
lies on the sheets and leaves
a smudge in the shape of a body,
nudges me awake and leads me
to the garden. *Here,* it says in a voice
I know though it's never spoken
to me before, *make your bed.*

A mole will visit, a night bird with a blizzard in its beak,
and something light as snow
will walk over you under your blanket of soil,

under the sky's forgetting. Something will walk over you
and something in the darkness that you finally own
will lie down.

Speak slowly with many pauses
            between
the words.

It's those pauses that are doing the work.

The one you cannot hear can hear them.

ARE THE ATOMS THAT MAKE UP YOUR BODY TRAVELLING AT THE SPEED OF DARKNESS TOWARD ANY KIND OF LIGHT?

Are you now resident of leaf, of beetle,
of river stone, of moon snail shell? A wasp

swallows part of you and spits you out
to make the paper for her paper nest.

It takes her weeks to build it, mouthful
by mouthful, saliva-wet. When it's dry

suspended like a long grey lung
from the cedar beam in the gazebo,

with a black felt pen I'll write
my name on it

so you'll remember me
and come back home.

WHAT I WISH I'D FIRST HEARD ON AWAKENING

Not birdsong though that will usually do,
not the coffee machine gurgling itself into morning,
not the oil furnace kicking in

Something quieter than that,
something capable of lifting
on its downy sound

only the wings of a mayfly,
only a tuft of cat hair caught
on the vellum shade of the lamp

What I wish I'd first heard
on awakening—beside me in our bed
a mouthful of air

WATERCOLOUR

Did you see the magnolia light its pink fires
inside the white, white blossoms?
You were gone before that first flush.
I don't know where you are now,
if you have a view of the garden like the one
we climbed the roof to see, bird's-eye, bat's-eye,
eye of passing cloud. The pond to me looks sad,
water lilies that opened in your poems flower once
and then give up, my fault perhaps. I don't know
if I'm to push into their soil a fertilizer tab
the size of a Tums that settles indigestion. I seem
to remember you did that when you waded in bare-chested
in your briefs, deleted expired buds and leaves,
your legs white as magnolia blossoms, and cold.
We had an eternity together.
Today it feels like just a day, dawn seeping into dusk
the minute the painter slides his wet brush
across the homemade paper. No pencil lines to separate
and make a difference, just water running into water
and becoming something else.

SEVEN WAYS TO KEEP ON GOING

1. Take on another language, an alphabet of bone and sinew and grit. Chew the gristle and learn by heart the songbook's oldest songs before you try to speak his name.

2. Draw his feet, long and elegant, the shape of them like slim trout. Take extra time with the toes you took into your mouth.

3. Find the word that means "the sky after a swan has flown through." A mute swan with wide white wings. The noun has been lost because too many fluent in this grasslands dialect, when they look up, see only emptiness.

4. Remember everything.
   (No, don't do that!)

5. The hawk and owl feathers he found in the fields and kept in a jar on his desk—glue them to the hollow near your shoulder blades where you once had wings. You can wear his leather jacket then and it won't look big.

6. Observe the ways of insects. An ant uses the body of another ant to build a bridge over the gap between the planks on the deck so he can get to where he needs to go.

7. Sleep on both sides of the bed. Confuse the cat.

SIX WAYS

1. Dry on the windowsill the wishbone of a snow goose. Make a wish without snapping it in two. That way what comes true will hold together.

2. To make friends with an Egyptian mare breathe into her nostrils. To make friends with crows walk past them with stiff legs as if you have no knees. To make friends with goats persuade your pupils to be horizontal so you can see what they see when you lie down.

3. Start a list of the things you didn't like about him.

Try harder.

4. Repeat after Lorca, "Light doesn't know what it wants." But its opposite does. Darkness wants the spark you've carried since your birth to illuminate its path. Otherwise, no matter where it goes, it can't find its way.

5. He broke almost every bone in his body. Count them: femur, ankle, wrist, collarbone, tibia, scapula, jaw, hip, pelvis. That's not almost every bone—there are 206 in the human skeleton. Still, that's a lot for one man. The breakage except for the ankle happened before you met. Try to figure out what that might mean.

6. Speak slowly with many pauses between the words. It's those pauses that are doing the work. The one you cannot hear can hear them.

FIVE WAYS

1. Sit down, stand up when it pleases you.

2. Tell the story about the ornithologist who pitched his research camp beyond the Arctic Circle. One morning he woke to a low fog hugging the snow-encrusted tundra. He stared into it from the doorway of his canvas hut. It wasn't fog but the breath of a thousand eiderdowns rising above their heads.

3. The heron didn't see its shadow in the water as a heron. Take note of this. The mirror on your dresser has drowned all images of the man who used to look into it every morning to comb his hair. Staring back at you, your face flat and shiny as fish scales sometimes holds a flicker that isn't you.

4. Build a House of Snow, a House of Memories, a House of Safe-Keeping, a House of Flutes. You can move between these houses but finally you'll have to choose. One is more comfortable than the other, one is cheaper, one more true. What furniture will you need, what provisions? Will anyone missing the earth, missing the domestic, come to help out with pots of geraniums, with paint chips and swatches? What door will you open to him? What door will you keep closed?

5. Sing only when the song is willing. Eat what pleases you. Breathe on the frozen salmon so it won't freeze the skin off your mouth and tongue.

FOUR WAYS

1. Talk to the turtle who burrows into the mud at the bottom of the pond for seven months and comes up quiet. Talk to the ants who eat your sugar nightly in the kitchen without making a sound. Talk to the stone that holds its emotions tight to its chest. You'll get used to no one joining in, no one answering. Now talk to the one who is gone. Say, *What a chill, what a wind.*

2. Prepare a sacrifice. Not something with blood in it but a mango, a plantain, an edible you're not used to. A potato therefore won't do. Maybe a durian. In Malaysia they say it stinks like hell and tastes like heaven. What could be better, bringing both afterworlds into the ritual? Though you don't like the smell of kerosene, light a kerosene lantern because that's what you used to bring into the room when the power went out, both of you sitting together, leaning into the amber glow, each with a different book in your hands, shoulders touching.

3. Make a breastplate against death, make a helmet against death, make a pair of steel-toed boots against death. But then you'll never find him. Walk naked and barefoot in the garden after dusk. Let the garter snake slide over your toes, let the owl swallow you with her eyes, let the night flowers sprinkle you with their listless pollen until you are invisible too.

4. Recite the saddest poem you know. It has only one word and it rhymes.

THREE WAYS

1. Learn to drive the lawn tractor. Wear his red John Deere cap with a crusty line of sweat around the inside brim. Get a farmer's tan. If the tractor tips on the slope and you're crushed under its weight, it will matter only for the hours you feel pain. Someone walking his dog will let her off the leash and she will find you. A working dog, shepherd or border collie, she will guide you to the Glade of the Fleshless. It won't smell of deliquescence but of freshly cut grass.

2. Some of the cloves of garlic he grew and hung in the shed to dry have turned to dust. That seems appropriate. Use them to flavour his ashes. Become that crazy woman in the newspaper who ate the remains of her husband a spoonful a day. Is this the taste of grief? Have you become a sorrow eater?

3. Buy a new mattress. Set the old one on fire in the back garden. You swear it looks like the flames are fucking. Wildly, without restraint. Throw in the fire the things you know he misses: his reading glasses, his carpenter's apron, the drum his friend made for him in prison. Add the screw that once held the bones of his ankle together when he jumped drunk and cocaine-crazy off a cliff into the Shuswap River. The screw is as long as your ring finger. Five years after the bones knit, it worked its way out through his skin. He may need it now. His ankle might have broken again on his leap out of this world into death's dark waters.

TWO WAYS TO KEEP ON GOING

1. Soon it will be over.
   Find the herb that grows on stone and brew it for a tea.
   It will make your heart turn hard.

2. Watch how water falls without breaking.
   Watch how snow falls without breaking.
   Watch how your cut hair falls to the floor and you lift your head.
   Your friends say how young you look.
   Look how light falls upon you and doesn't break.

Look at how light falls upon you
and doesn't break.

IT'S THE DARKNESS OF YOUR OWN HEART HEALING

At midnight everything in the house
turns off its light: the porcelain
vase on the hall table, the cherrywood floor,
the glass of milk by the stove, the fever lantern
placed on the trunk at the end of the bed.
Does he come to you in dreams?
Everything at midnight turns off its light.

WINTER JASMINE

By December your many souls
were halfway to being
somewhere else. But the body?

It didn't want to leave
the winter jasmine
opening its star-like blossoms
outside the bedroom door.
It didn't want to leave the stale
grey robe it rarely shrugged off
or the smell of coffee
though the taste no longer
jazzed the mouth.

The souls were pleased you left
your shorn hair on a branch
for the nest of the hummingbirds
who stayed all winter.
They were pleased the cat
was sleeping on your chest,
the body so still beneath her purring
she didn't want to move.

Muddled from the medicine
and too much sleep, almost
invisible to itself, the body
didn't think to tell you
the souls were calling
and no matter how much you loved
the small change of the earth
rubbed to a lustre in your inner pocket
it had to go.

THE FIRST NIGHT

The first night of the Cold Moon.
Rising in the east, it lays its eye on me.
I am barely here, part of me
gone with my dead husband though I'm not
refined enough to know where that is
or what I'm seeing beyond his pale
drug-swollen face. In the garden
the chilled air quills me
with frost, head to toe, it rimes
my lips. Even if I knew what to say
I couldn't say it, I am wintered
with woe, I am flensed, my bones
moving to the surface their stunned
cold-moon glare.

FORESTS BURNING TO THE NORTH

Running on the road,
opening my mouth,
inhaling—

my tongue startles—

it's the taste of you
when you used to smoke
a pack and a half a day.

1. Take home an African grey from the Parrot Rescue Society. Don't teach him your words; learn the squeaks and squawks of parrot talk. If you turn up the music and bob around his cage, he'll nod his head, shrug his shoulders, lift one foot then the next, flap his wings. When he sees Björk on TV in her swan dress, the long cygnus neck draped over her shoulder, the head and beak bumping into her right breast, he goes berserk. To please him you wear a shift of chicken feathers, of mango peels, of raw meat.

2. Stand at the end of your driveway early Monday morning as if you just happen to be there clad in your bathrobe, demurely closed. Soon the man who drives the neighbourhood on this same day once a week will jump from the doorway of his big truck to the road. Look surprised to see him and begin your flirtation. Make sure your garbage tied tightly, a modest bag from a single household, smells enticing and bold.

3. Invent a new religion based entirely on light. No gods or parables, just sunlight on a page, moonlight riding waves into the shore, candlelight flickering inside a lantern. The cathedral is a clearing in the trees, a mountaintop, a river delta. The only words you borrow are "Let there be light." The rest is silence, openness, and glow. In such a religion, even the dead immortally shine.

HUSBAND, I SAID

Last night you called to me.
You were somewhere in the garden
and I had to find you. Should I count
to ten? Our garden was bigger than before,
so much emptiness where you used to be.
Look up, I thought you said. I was hoping
for a brown bat. What I saw was
the moon, white and thin as a toenail clipping.
Has all romance gone out of me?
Husband? I said. The sound of water
from the waterfall in the pond, a whistle
from a rat in the compost bin. After sunset
the beans and peas don't climb the net
you wove from string between the bamboo poles.
Among the vegetables it's only darkness
that is rising. It makes
the sound of growing hair.

DEATH LIES DOWN BESIDE ME

There's no light in the room,
I can't see his face,
but the must of his breath
moistens the back of my neck
and his arm falls across my shoulder
with the sure weight
of a shovelful of earth.

It doesn't feel bad, his being here.
He's chosen my bed the way a dog
chooses the bed of his favourite in the family.
The room a little cold, the wind night-walking,
soon his breathing matches mine.

How is this different from my husband
sleeping beside me? How is this different
from my husband running his finger
down my spine to wake me up?

Pancakes for breakfast,
pig's feet or marrow bones—what is it
come morning death claims
he wants?

WE DIDN'T SAY

You leave me
in this drought-
stricken time
a well of silence.

I lower a pail on a rope
and pull it up, hand over hand,
dip a tin cup inside its darkness,
raise it to my lips and swallow.

I've been so thirsty since.

The taste is iron,
as hard and old as that,
the taste is alkali
and no one talking.

The words we didn't say
go bad in the mouth.
They weigh down my tongue,
dulled and ugly as a dead fish.

SHATTER

My glasses, my running shoes,
three oranges in a bag,
my watch with the wide red strap,
my purse, my phone, messages of
love and anger, everything gets lost,
more often, without respite.

Is this because of the bigger loss?

Who knew a windshield, that solid
impermeable thing, when it shatters
becomes a thousand pellets of glass?

This metaphor's not good enough
but you know what I mean,
if you've been there,
if you're looking, still looking,
you know what I mean.

The hawk and owl feathers he found in the fields
and kept in a jar on his desk—glue them
to the hollow near your shoulder blades
where you once had wings. You can wear
his leather jacket then and it won't look big.

A RARE SNOW IN THE RAINFOREST

Flake after flake, snow
builds a small exquisite drift

on the beak
of the pine siskin.

A puff of fog hangs
in front of his face—

I've never seen it before—
a bird's breath!

FORGIVENESS

That ant mound
baked hard in the sun
could be death's helmet.

Why not, with his affinity
for insects—the bluebottle, the blow,
all the Coleoptera and more?

And he'd be okay
with most of him
underground

only the top of his head
visible
above the golden foxtails.

Perhaps it's just his helmet
dropped in the grass
and he's gone

for a walkabout.
Look for bone-tracks in the fallow,
the long skull of a horse,

scat the colour
of old blood.
There's so much

to atone for.
Only death
with his insect jaws

his hard
snout, has it in him
to forgive.

POEM AND REFLECTION

The mirror
shows time

yet doesn't keep it:

so must I
live only

the now
in me

not the past
unhoured

as I am
from you

DRYER THAN THIS

An invisible fire in the grass
crackles underfoot.
We need you more than ever.

Among other things, you were
a dowser. Walking the land
with a willow wand

you could feel the water
in your hands you said,
but couldn't tell

if it was spoiled or sweet.
This afternoon the sky
spat once and weakly

like a boy
just learning how
to spit. Today I rubbed

the last of you
between thumb and index finger,
brought you to my lips.

The soil between
the rows of wheat burned thin,
is greyer, dryer than this.

THE BREATH OF HEAVEN

1.
My tongue is my mother, my throat
my father. I would sing for you if I could,
I would tap my teeth with a tuning fork.

2.
The hand of god tosses crystal stones into the water.
The pool takes on a thousand eyes.

Now everything looks at you.

I see a star overhead start over.
Its new name is Afterlight.

The moon's sails fill with the breath of heaven.

I would sing for you
if my tongue were my own,
if my teeth didn't chatter.

3.
A dragonfly's wings make that same sound,
that clicking like cuspids
on a string.

4.
The *Book of Forgetting*
        is buried with the body.
The dead too want to read.

You scrawl your name on the title page.
An act of bravado. You want to be known
        down under.

5.

In the Library of Alexandria,
the writing on a wall of scrolls
            in English means
the place for the cure of the soul.

The library the wasps built on the beams
of the gazebo—it too gets set on fire.

Now all the souls in the garden
        cover themselves with ash—

they are as visible
        as your own skin
                on a night without stars.

SMALL LESSON

Hoarfrost feathering the window
and behind that a high cloud
and behind that the hunter's moon.

Three things without
a light inside them
yet how they shine.

BEFORE YOU KNOW WHAT LOVE IS

you must lose it, you must walk into a room
and he won't be there, not ever,
he's not gone to the store, he's not having coffee
with his brother at the local café. His truck sits
in the driveway and no one drives it, his robe on a hook behind the door
is shedding the smell of him—the mud in the treads of his boots
petrifies, the food he cooked and froze,
bag after bag of tomato sauce, his failed lasagna,
his chicken stew and rhubarb pie, they outlast, how can you eat them,
how can you throw them out?
You must lose him over and over again; then
something you didn't expect might unlock the door,
raise the blind, and flip the sign from Closed to Open.
And through the windows once so smeared no one could look out or in
light now streams as if the girl who specialized
in cleaning windows to pay her way through theatre school
scrubbed and polished the glass until the nothing
you could see inside the sad and empty places
is more than the sun parsing the absences
and you walk into it
and something close to love
is waiting

FALLEN ANGELS

Many spend their days
as you might expect
raising the fallen:

the wooden panel fence
on the south side of the barnyard,
the naked fledgling,
the woman with torn stockings
who hobbles from streetlamp
to streetlamp, a broken heel
on one shoe.

Some fall again
knocked down by wind
by rivalry
by need.

The angels do it over
in spite of.
They have time.

Even the apples
they reattach,
even the tears.

DON'T SEPARATE

Moss from stone
I from thou
the river from the sea—

you still come to me
in beauty   in sickness

your sour mouth
singing

Walk naked and barefoot in the garden after dusk.
Let the garter snake slide over your toes,
let the owl swallow you with her eyes,
let the night flowers sprinkle you with their dark listless
until you are invisible too.

THE WAY OF THINGS

The large six-gilled shark
who lived in the deepest
waters of the bay, therefore
rarely seen,
washed up on the beach.

Our neighbour found it,
a picture appeared in the paper
and people from the city gathered.

A small boy poked its eye
with a stick. I asked him
to stop, to show it some respect.
His father yelled at me.

You were sick in bed
in our house across the road.
I tried to describe the shark.
You didn't want to hear.

The next day the paper said
a biologist from the university
necropsying the fish in situ
found babies in her belly.
She may have died trying to give birth.
After you had gone, months after,
I went back.

Small bones nested inside larger ones,
the tides pulling them over the stones
then pushing them back, the bones
fleshless because of the roll,
the gulls, and the rot,

it is the way of things.

BELIEVE

The stars are made of salt.
Scatter them on your country road
to melt the ice. There are stars enough
for all the winters ahead of you.
And the roses in July outside your door?
They want to be eaten. That's why
they look at you so brazenly,
without shame. They speak directly
to your teeth and gut. What else
should you add to your self-help notes
for the out-of-sorts, the unblessed, the afflicted?
Dust can be shaped into a comely
loaf of bread. It just needs some spit
and two good hands to believe in it—
it will surely rise—

THE WAITING

I was waiting for something
to arrive. Something that travelled
on water, on moonlight
drenched by the tide, something

wet and brackish. I could
taste it, smell it,
though I didn't know its name.
This was the first time in months

that blood memory
pulsed between my legs,
the first time my breasts felt tongued.
Old woman, widow,

I didn't know what I wanted,
didn't know
what was moving my way
across the water, I didn't expect

a prophet or a saviour walking his miracle
from wave to wave, I was sitting quiet
listening to the tide come in,
crooked fingers in my lap,

the bent and dry of me wanting
to be rolled and tumbled on the beach,
a baptism of weal and woe,
a wild unbecoming.

WHEN YOU WERE A DOG, WERE YOU HAPPY?

Some days I am more dog
                    than me;

when I hear a vole breathing
                    underground

when the heat stays in my hair

when a smell flies like a frenzied bird
                    and whacks me on the head,
the cortex flashing *squirrel, bitch, rotten fish*

when I don't know what *suspicious*
means
                    or *deceit* or *eternity*

I can't laugh as a dog
                    but my whole body mimics laughter—
if this were charades you'd get it

And when I check my canine, un-
canny clock and know your truck's
                    about to turn into the driveway

                    I'm at the door, my lip curled up,
my doggy face grinning

WHAT'S IT LIKE?

Going slowly on wooden skis
and the snow falling

The snow under the skis,
the frozen breath

of a village
dreaming underground,

among the sleepers
the one you lost—his breath

you creak across
going slowly

through the darkness of the pines

ONE WAY TO KEEP ON GOING

Apply to be the Minister
                    of the Ministry of Loneliness.
The qualifications are as follows: you must live alone (cats but not
dogs are allowed); you must present, in concrete form, evidence
of your suitability (e.g., an empty dayminder, liquor store receipts,
many reservations for a table for one); you must possess a univer-
sity degree preferably in nineteenth-century Russian literature;
you must know the words of five melancholy songs by heart, each
of which includes at least one of the following: a whippoorwill, a
bottle of whisky, the whistle of a freight train, a gravel road, a
stoop, a jail cell, last call. You must swear in writing that you dance
in the kitchen on your own, that you lay one place setting at the
table for the evening meal. There is a space at the end of the job
application to add a personal touch. For instance, you could say
that from the front porch you watched the last person who will
love you walking into the woods in falling snow. The stars were
falling too. The birch trees, white as bones, stepped forward to
take him in.

NOTES

The title "What Is the Most You Can Ask of Air?" is from Karen Enns, "Notes for the Angel's Descent," *That Other Beauty.*

The first line of "Watercolour" comes from Elizabeth Austen, "This Morning," *Every Dress a Decision.*

The title "It's the Darkness of Your Own Heart Healing" is a line from Yves Bonnefoy's "The Tree, the Lamp."

The title and first line of "The Waiting" come from a poem of the same title by Jane Wong.

Some of these poems have appeared in the journals *Exile, Arc, Freefall, Riddle Fence, Nimrod,* and *The Literary Review of Canada,* and in the anthology *The Path to Kindness.* "Inside a Needle" was printed on the panel of a fish truck in Woody Point, Newfoundland, in 2019.

Arc produced a broadside of "In Lieu of Flowers" and the composer, Leslie Uyeda, set several of these poems to music.

ACKNOWLEDGEMENTS

My last book, a prose memoir called *Through the Garden: A Love Story (with Cats)*, focused on my husband Patrick Lane's illness and the highlights of the forty years we spent with each other and our five cats. I began the book when Patrick started to experience a number of strange symptoms, which side-stepped any diagnosis, and ended it three years later with him still alive. The writing of our story kept me going through the hours of care-taking, sadness, and worry.

Patrick died in 2019, a year before the memoir's publication. Almost immediately after, I began editing a small collection of poems he'd left behind. Called *The Quiet in Me*, it came out with Harbour Press in 2022. Also, after his death, I turned back to my own poetry and tried to voice the heartbreaking grief that left me almost numb. As it has in the past, poetry, along with the love of friends, is what saved me. I see this book as a companion piece to the memoir and to Patrick's posthumous poems. In my mind the books comprise a trilogy that I believe he'd be pleased to be a part of.

It was a blessing to share a good part of my life with this special man and brilliant writer. I see now that such a writing companionship continues after death. These poems, I hope, are a testament to love's everlastingness. I hope too that they strike a match that will be visible in the darkness that the bereaved, whoever they may be, must travel through.

So many were there for me, especially Patrick's sons Richard and Michael Lane, and the six grandchildren. In addition to them, I want to thank Rhonda Ganz, Tina Biello, Alexander Pohran Dawkins, and Elizabeth Philips. Also Lynda Haverstock, Susan Olding, Seán Virgo, Eric McCormack, Susan Musgrave, Mary McGovern, and lately, Tom O'Flanagan.

My deepest gratitude goes to the composer Leslie Uyeda for her inspired interpretation of my poems over the years, particularly her brilliant musical cycle "When I Stop Saying Your Name," based on five selections from this collection. The world premiere took place on March 23, 2023, in Celebration Hall at Mount Pleasant Cemetery in Vancouver.

After That owes its presence in the world to the warm, supportive folks at McClelland & Stewart, in particular Kelly Joseph, Ruta Liormonas, Canisia Lubrin, and Talia Abramson. The copy editor, Heather Sangster, has lent her sharp eye to my poetry over many years and the poems are better for her close attention.

Finally, I want to thank those of you who hold this book in your hands. Supporters of poetry are rare and refined, and much appreciated. You complete the full circle of the poem from the time of its inception until its meeting with the ones who let it into their lives.

© Rafal Gerszak

LORNA CROZIER is the author of the memoir *Through the Garden*, which was named a *Globe and Mail* Top 100 Book and a finalist for the Hilary Weston Writers' Trust Prize for Nonfiction and the City of Victoria Butler Book Prize. She has published eighteen books of poetry, including *God of Shadows*, *What the Soul Doesn't Want*, *The Wrong Cat*, *Small Mechanics*, *The Blue Hour of the Day: Selected Poems*, and *Whetstone*. She is also the author of the memoir *Small Beneath the Sky*, which won the Hubert Evans Award for Creative Nonfiction. She won the Governor General's Literary Award for Poetry for *Inventing the Hawk* and three additional collections were finalists for this award. She has received the Canadian Authors Association Award, three Pat Lowther Memorial Awards, the Raymond Souster Award, and the Dorothy Livesay Poetry Prize. She was awarded the BC Lieutenant Governor's Award for Literary Excellence, the George Woodcock Lifetime Achievement Award, and the Kloppenburg Award for Literary Excellence. She is a Professor Emerita at the University of Victoria and an Officer of the Order of Canada, and she has received five honorary doctorates for her contributions to Canadian literature. Born in Swift Current, Saskatchewan, she now lives in British Columbia.